VIC BOTT
Interviewed by Mike

During the 1980s, Mike Johnson made interesting Redditch people. We have now decided to present the material from the videos as a series of booklets. This first publication covers the life and times of Vic Bott.

Vic was born in 1898 and came to live in Redditch when he was six years old. Ten years later he lied about his age and enlisted in the Worcestershire Regiment. After serving there for a year, he was transferred to the newly-formed Machine Gun Corps, fighting on the front line in France and Belgium. On demobilisation he joined Royal Enfield as 'the lowest of the low' but rose to become one of their senior managers. He died just before his 100th birthday. Vic was well-known for his paintings and sketches.

Mike Johnson: *You were born in 1898, during the time of the Boer War in South Africa. And you have lived through the reign of Queen Victoria, Edward VII, George V, Edward VIII, George VI and Queen Elizabeth II, spanning some 75 years. But you weren't born in Redditch, you were born in Cheltenham and you moved to Redditch when you were six years old. What are your memories of coming to Redditch?*

Vic Bott: A complete change inasmuch as the house we had in Cheltenham was on a main road where the trams ran, my first impression of Redditch was that it was like going into the country. We stayed in Britten Street with my grandfather until dad had got established and found a house to bring the family up in. We set up home in Albert Street which was a cul-de-sac. And from then on, I fell in love with Redditch.

Albert Street bordered on the Bartlett estate which stretched from the top of Prospect Hill to the beginning of Albert Street, and the whole length of Albert Street on the right hand side. Going back to the top of Prospect Hill, it included the whole of Easemore Road to where Lady Harriet Lane starts. Stretching along the whole length of Albert Street was a wood belonging to Mr Bartleet, of beautiful standard timber, beech trees - like a little forest in a way, The boundary to all our gardens – we had fairly long gardens – was brick walls that we used to climb very often and play cowboys and indians in the wood. Invariably the old gentleman Bartlett used to walk about, and when he captured us he used to escort us up to the Coach House and give us a lecture, saying what a terrible thing we'd done, trespassing on his property.

Everybody was needle-making or in the allied trades. We were a population of about 25,000 in them days, and most were self-employed. My grandad, I remember him, he was quite a character he was about six foot (nearly two metres) and about 70 plus, he had got a mass of white hair, a big droopy moustache, broad shoulders, and he'd always got two pigs in the sty. He used to have a bench in that house and he did fish-hook filing, filing the barbs on hooks. He'd work three days a week and then go fox hunting.

This is how it worked. You would buy a roll of wire, I would cut it to lengths, Joe Smith would point it, somebody else would straighten it, it went through about seven hands and then it came back to where it started from. Then it was packed up and despatched with a company name and perhaps it was only a few neighbours working together.

The Birmingham Road went straight through to Birmingham in those days, didn't it?

Birmingham Road started as a built-up area at the end of Clive Road. And directly opposite Clive Road was a gate which led to two meadows that took you straight up to Forge Mill. Forge Mill consisted in them days of the big house which is still in existence, and was held by the Wright family. And then on the opposite side to the Wright mansion was Forge Mill, derelict except for the scouring mill which was on the ground floor. It was a two-storey building and the first floor was derelict, there was no access to it except for a rotting eight-door stairway which only started halfway up.

The Hunt family, who I believe originated in Alcester, were running the scouring mill. They had three sons, they were big friends of me and my brother, we formed a club and the top storey of this derelict building was our clubhouse. But you took your life in your hands to get up there. The eldest boy, Clarrie, he was a genius type of bloke, he afterwards did very well in Australia, he fixed up a block and tackle and a bosun's chair attachment and you were hoisted up to the top if you were a member.

Horses would play a big part in your youth. Would all the traders have a horse and wagon?

Loading the cart at Forge Mill. .One of Norman Neasom's lovely drawings.

Everybody seemed to have a different type of horse in those days. The local baker, Mr Salmon, had a Welsh cob. He used to do his baking and when he'd finished his baking he'd take the bread round, it used to be delivered to your door in those days. His shop was an ordinary little front shop, a grocer's shop and he sold everything there, sugar, tea - it was the Sainsbury's of the old days. Mr Attwood was a confectioner at the top of Fish Hill, he had three conveyances and an Arab type of pony, it was very small, I would say about ten hands. Then the doctors, Dr Smith and Dr Stephenson, they had cobs, Welsh cobs with a trap. Then Brown, Hopwood & Gilbert, which was the main grocery wholesalers from Birmingham, used to come about twice a week, four-in-hands, they were a Suffolk, Punch type of horse.

The majority of goods into Redditch came by rail in those days and at the bottom of Unicorn Hill was a big depot. The distribution from those goods yards to the various factories and shops was done with a flat dray and a Clydesdale horse. That meant that they had to face a hill whichever way they went. If they went up Oakly Road that was a hill, if they went up Unicorn Hill, that was a hill, if they went up Bates Hill, that was a hill, but the Unicorn Hill was the main entrance to the town. On the left hand side concrete serrations were put so that a horse could get a foothold, and a boy was always stationed at the bottom with a spare trace horse to hitch on to the vehicle so that the drivers were able to take it to the top.

The drivers were real characters. They knew everybody, they knew all the answers and all the tricks of the trade. By 11 oclock and 12 o'clock opening time they'd done half a day's work, because they had to get up in the morning, see to the horse, harness him, get there and then load up with goods. One man's round would be Oakly Road, Park Road, Evesham St, Alcester St and back down to the station. There's one old chap always used to call in the Railway pub regular (probably the Little Railway, now the Golden Cross). The horse stopped, 'Whoa!', the door opened and his pint was there on the counter waiting for him. He'd drink it down, 'Morning Missus' and he'd be away. There's something called 'mothers' that you sometimes get in the ale, a deposit of sorts in the brewing of it I should imagine, but anyway, the story is told that he went through the usual procedure, 'Whoa', door opened, pint on the counter, 'mornin missus' then he added 'A few mothers in it this morning'. The door slammed and off he went.

It was a drunken age then, no doubt about it then. A pint of beer was about tuppence three halfpence (ie 2d+1.5d=3.5d = 1.4 new pence), something like that and a nip of rum was about tuppence (less than 1p). You could get sozzled on a tanner (6d - just over 2p). A lot of people came from Headless Cross, Crabbs Cross, Ipsley and it was reckoned that if employers could get them past the Vine (in Evesham Street, on the corner of Worcester Road) in the morning they would do a day's work.

That colossol wage of eighteen pence (just over 7p) was a lot of money in those days. Halfpennies were something and a farthing was important.

The houses in Peakmen Street have all gone now. What was the street like in your young days?

The National School built in about 1840, which later became St Stephen's. The photo is courtesy Redditch library and is listed Peakman St school but is definitely the old National School.

They were terraced houses, nondescript really in modern terms but very comfortable. Most of the tradesmen lived there. In those days the shops were all private traders. Peakman Street was one of the main streets of Redditch, Ipsley Street was another but Archer Road and Other Road were only a scattering of houses, they weren't built up at all. The main buildings were St Stephens school, the infants school and the lady's school. The girls school and the infants school was on the left-hand side of Peakman Street

You went to school at St Stephens which was on the corner of Peakman Street and Archer Road. What do you remember about those days?

I remember my mother taking me to the infant school in Peakman Street and settling me down in the class and much to my astonishment, both the headmistress of the infants school and her sister, who was a teacher, were named Bott. Whether that was to her annoyance or not I don't know, but the earliest recollection I've got of the infant school was a blow on top of my head with a slate for using a screeching slate pencil. The pencil was made of slate and occasionally there was something like a diamond embedded in the contents, and if you used your pencil too hard it made a terrible screeching noise like the railway engines' top button blaster. There were no books, they were all slates, and you had to use your pocket handkerchief to wipe off.

The classes went from one to seven, class seven was the excel. I loved school and I was always in the first six. That was bribery and corruption because Mrs Treadgold taught from class one up to four and if the lads attained top of the class she gave them sixpence and I remember we were all after the tanner. I think she was the senior woman teacher, she was a matron and I think she was distantly related to the Treadgold family who ran the cinema.

Now one of the little gems of democracy in Redditch was St Stephen's school. I'd only got one pair of trousers, one pair of boots and I think they were made of cardboard. I was sat next to a kid whose dad was Watkins, the confectioners, or his dad might have been a superintendent at Henry Milward whose family had enough money to go round, because there was no higher education in Redditch. There was only one school so we were all mixed up together and that was true democracy.

This generation has never experienced the kind of poverty that existed in those days.

People ask, 'How did you exist?'. Well, as they say comparisons are odious. If you're poor and I'm poor and he's poor and they're poor you would say my poorness doesn't affect me because you are poorer.

But it astounds me. We were poor, nearly every family in Redditch was, of course, everybody had got an uneconomical family. In short, my mother never went out to work, we were a family of three, then a family of five and we finished up a family of seven. My dad was a skilled bloke, a craftsman, he could make a reel as well as a rod and I think he would be on about £3 a week. Three pounds a week! How the hell could you manage? I'm not holding it against my dad, as far as I was concerned, my dad was one of the most important blokes in the world. But I mean, wasn't it wrong? What chance had a kid? Second or none. My elder brother was ever so clever, but he died when he was 23 as a result of the war. Now I reckon he'd have been a real clever bloke but they couldn't afford a pencil or a compass. As for meals, it had to be filling, not taste, bulk. They were mainly cabbage and vegetables. As long as you had a tummy full you was alright.

In those days, children were expected to make some contribution to the family income when they were as young as ten. Many children were associated with one or other of the little factories in the area and ran errands for the management. I was an errand boy first when I was about 12, I worked for Laight's in Edward Street. You know the railway bridge, where Morralls were, that used to be a big garden and there were two cottages that belonged to Laights, I forget their trade name I think their trademark was a snake. They were needle factors, they'd got a business and and their own trade name and everything but all they did was burnish the needles. They finished the needles and they packed them. There used to be a place at the top of Bates Hill where the bloke did nothing else but tea chests. All the needles were put in for export, then you'd send your quota - I'd put in mine for Laight's, then the tin smiths would solder everything up to stop humidity and all that, they called it Tropicalisation,

As I grew older I sought a more suitable and lucrative part-time job. At that time (about 1912) Mrs Treadgold had just introduced the first cinematograph shows at the church road entertainment centre and she required the services of 'two bright lads' to sell chocolates during the interval. I was one of those appointed on the recommendation of the headmaster. The films tended to be either Cowboys and Indians or the 'Bessie the Dog' kind and only lasted about ten minutes. Mrs Treadgold used to pad them out with conjurers and other entertainers. These shows drew a larger audience than those put on by the Temperance Hall which usually depicted a dying young girl with a drunken father - you went in an exuberant youth and came out depressed.

The old cinema is still standing at Crabbs Cross, until recently it was Samuel Latham's brush factory. It was built in the 1890s as a leisure centre for Royal Enfield workers from the factory in Hunt End. Note the two Royal Enfield cars outside. Royal Enfield were making cars from about 1896 to 1908.

In the early days of the cinema, a two-reel film was quite something. Mrs Treadgold was originally in Church Road but when her lease expired there she built 'the Select' (in Alcester Street). She also leased another cinema at Crabbs Cross, the building is still there on the Evesham Road, now called the Samuel Latham Brush Factory, it's opposite the the little primary school and by the pedestrian crossing. She rented the films off Pathe, it was shown in Redditch then I'd take that up to Crabbs Cross for a showing there on my bike.

Apart from the cinema, the entertainment was all local talent. Very rarely you got outside talent in Redditch. The main societies were The Dickens Fellowship, the Redditch Amateur Dramatic Society, and the Redditch Opera Company. That was exclusive, they built up their name as a first class opera company, performing in the Old Public Hall in Church Road. If you were in the Redditch Opera Company, that was a distinction.

You left school at thirteen years old and you went to work at Bartletts. But you didn't enjoy it, did you?

When you were first employed at thirteen you were just a link in a very big chain – you were the butt of everybody. I remember my first job there was assembling what they called Archer's spin-a-fin. It was two metal rings attached to the eye of a large needle and they used to impregnate a dead minnow and as it was brought through the water the spin used to rotate it. I had the wonderful technology of assembling the rings of the spin-a-fin. I worked from 8 in the morning until 12, and 2 to 5 plus Saturday morning for eighteen pence a week (18d ie just over 7d).

I stopped at Bartletts for twelve months, then I went to Alcock's which was a step up the ladder. They were one of the major employers in Redditch, male and female. Most of the ladies were employed on the fly dressing, a very skilled job, the girls had to serve an apprenticeship of about three years. It was a long shop about 12 foot wide and 30 yards long (approx 3.5 metres x 17.5 metres). It was a long building, facing on to Clive Road and there were small mullioned windows. The light was not very good. There were 12 gas burners, no mantle, just a flat burner with a Stayflame. The only heating in that place was three ordinary stoves and those stoves had to be lit by errand boys from the Lodge. They had all these gorgeous feathers, birds of Paradise and all types, and they used wax to attach the feathers to the body of the fly. The wax had to be warm so to keep it warm they invariably sat on the wax or put it under their arms.

To start in that organisation as a male juvenile you had to start in the Lodge. Your duties in the Lodge was running errands for everybody, fetching the post in the morning, taking it during the daytime, getting sticks to prepare the fires for the various departments for fly dressing, and everybody's dogsbody. There were four boys employed in the Lodge and seniority was by age and me being the eldest, I was the senior.

Now the Lodge was controlled by the commissionaire, at that time a chap named Bob Kings, a tall, very distinguished-looking bloke but a strict disciplinarian. I liked him tremendously even though he was instrumental in getting me the sack but I've never held it against him. When the commissionaire went to his lunch, which was after the ordinary workers, the senior boy at the Lodge used to sit at the desk at the little wicket window and the workers had to pass the window and if they were late. You had to put their name down, they were fined so much and that was stopped out of their wages. But if they were a dark-haired, attractive female, I just said 'Hullo' and put my pencil down.

Bob Kings who was a strict disciplinarian. The Lodge had to be absolutely spotless and on a Saturday morning it was our duty, in turns, to get on our hands and knees and scrub that floor. Although they were ordinary floorboards they were almost white with the continual scrubbing. One Saturday morning, we had done that, I had just finished that and was very pleased with my efforts when the Mr Kings walked in. Whether somebody had upset him or not I don't know, he scowled and said that he wasn't satisfied and I had got to do it again. I was very indignant. I told him, no, I wasn't going to do it again, I had made a good job of it. He gave me a cuff and said, 'Cheeky young devil'. I flung the floorcloth at him, I don't know what made me do it, it's quite against my ordinary way of life, anyway I let him have it and it curled round his neck and spoiled his beautiful white collar. I was waiting for a body blow but to my astonishment he burst out laughing. Then his strict discipline came into force and I was marched up to a little department where there was a very elderly gentleman with a beard (probably Mr Maynard), who sat me down and gave me a severe lecture about going against discipline and all that. I thought I had got away with it because he was talking to me in a fatherly way but the sum total was, 'Victor, I think you'll have to go'. And that was the end of my career at Samuel Alcock.

That was two jobs in a little over twelve months. Then I went to work at Thomas's, in Albert Street. We were supposed to be apprenticed to toolmaking but first you had to work a machine, you worked your way up in various stages but the ultimate aim was toolmaking really. They were making the charger clip, that was the magazine for five .303 bullets, the magazines, for the Lee Enfield .303 rifle.

We are now approaching the start of the 1914-18 war and you volunteered to join the army. What age were you when you signed up?

I was just sixteen years and five months. (Vic told them he was seventeen). We were all issued with a card to say that we were on munitions and we weren't therefore supposed to join the services but my workmates and I - we rebelled. I must have been a cheeky so-and-so in them days. The recruiting office was where on the corner of George Street and Front Hill, by the clockmaker. I don't know what the shop was, an old draper's shop of some sorts but it was on Front Hill, anyway, the third shop from the beginning of George Street.

We were among about 60 new recruits who accepted the king's shilling. The band took us down to the station, everybody wished us farewell and when we got to Worcester there was a lot of palaver there and we were back in Redditch! It must have been something to do with the overloading of too many recruits. Then we were sent back and we had a day at Silver Street barracks at Worcester, afterwards we were dispersed to various places – we were sent to Pershore and we were in private billets there.

We were posted to the Worcestershire regiment. It was chaotic in the early days. It was a long time before we had any equipment or khakis. There were so many people joining up you didn't know whether you were in the Worcestershire or the Glorius Gloucesters but we were part of a feeder. Now the feeder was to the first eight and to the second eight which was two regular territorial battalions, and they were in the 48th territorial division. The battalion I was with was sent up to Catterick. At Catterick the machine gun corps was being formed as a corps just like the artillery – we had big transport but instead of having guns we had limbers and the limbers was two boxes, joined by an ordinary connection, four horse teams, two drivers, rear and fore. Ammunition was our big job, with guns firing 600 rounds a minute you've got to have some ammunition. Recruits were sent from the various infantry battalions to form this now corps. So there was Worcestershire, Warwickshire, Oxfordshire, Buckinghamshire, Scottish regiments, the Naval Brigade, Australians, New Zealanders and so on.

We finished out training at Grantham and Madresfield then we went to a transit camp at Etaples in France which was more like a concentration camp. It was the lousiest camp in the British army, full of yellow bellies – guardsmen. We were supposed to be fully trained when we went to Etaples and you spent three days on all the paper work, where you'd be assigned to and what battalion you were sent to and what division they were and all that, and all the time you'd be going over the same drill. They were a lot of sadistic soldiers.

So the time would come when you would be ready to move up to the front line. What do you remember of that?

We were a detail of two, I remember. Me being the senior I had got all the paperwork. Our job was to go to the railhead and get in touch with the railway transport officer. He was in charge of transporting wherever your papers told you you had got to go, and seeing that you got there. You were approaching the front line then, about ten miles away from that actual activity. Then you were sent to a forward position which was usually company-held brigade headquarters or the battalion that was in the line or due to be in the line. You had to wait for a ration party, that was chaps with sandbags, tin hats and what-have-you moving into the line, when circumstances permitted, to get the food for those people in the trenches, and then you would tack yourself on to the ration party that was going to the particular unit that you was assigned to. Unfortunately, in our particular case, it was the night of a big counter attack by Jerry and the chap who was with me, a chap named Cracknell, he had only been in the trenches a day and he was captured. I lost sight of him until the war was over.

Two photographs from the front line of WW1. Both are badly creased and Vic evidently carried them round in his pocket.
All WW1 pictures courtesy Vic Bott's daughter.

The first night of the bombardment I was absolutely rigid with terror, (he couldn't move and thought he would be shot for cowardice). It's indescribable. The shells are flying around. It was absolutely terrifying. You can't call it cowardice, it's something to do with shattering your nerves. You were absolutely rigid. That lasted for nearly a fortnight before you got anywhere near accustomed to it. But afterwards you became more or less adjusted to it. When you come to weigh it up, the resilience of human beings, what they can stand, is out of this world.

At the start of each day you would be assigned to a team. The company was the usual set-up, sections, four sections to a company, four companies to a battalion. We always used to be a machine gun company, not a battalion, and

A lighter moment off duty. Vic sits on a covered chair, perhaps meant to be some kind of throne, and the soldiers from left to right carry a broom, a tray with drinks, and a soda syphon while the last one on the right has a saw. It's impossible to see what Vic is holding but the bag below reads 'Office Mess'.

Taken from a painting of the front line by Vic, initially presented to the British Legion Club, but now in the family's possession.

you were sent to whatever brigade your company was assigned to. You would mix with the infantry then. This was static trench warfare. Your officer would allocate a position for you, a machine gun position, a static position. There was usually a dugout built into the side for so many men, and you were two hours on duty (manning the gun) and four hours off. When you were off, you just kept your head down or you were doing some menial task in the trenches, more often than not manning the pump to drain the water away. Everybody got called to do that, they were manual pumps. From long long past when Gerry had advanced across the plains of Belgium and France, what he couldn't take he flooded. So we was in the flood area and he was on the higher ground. That was pretty well the situation during all the First World War.

Vic carried a small drawing pad round with him and made sketches in off-duty periods. This is of a German pill box showing that a direct hit had left the dug-out intact.

Another of Vic's sketches, taken from his front line note pad!

Trench feet was a terrible bloody disease in those days. We had got no waders, they were unheard of. Wellingtons wasn't thought about either. You just went in ordinary shoes and puttees. With Trench foot your feet looked like tripe - sickly, white, serrated. We treated it with whale oil and the smell of that was worse than the condition of your legs.

Sleeping was a haphazard affair, you would catnap when you could but you daren't catnap when you were stood to. That was a heinous offence. You daren't sleep on your post, the maximum penalty was death.

How long we spent on the line at one time depended on circumstances, it should have been seven to eight days but if there was an attack or a counter attack or circumstances such as intense barrages when you were supposed to be relieved, the relief would be cancelled.

A candle was a necessity. When you were coming out of the trenches, cleaning up and that, we were all lousy and the seams of your trousers and your vest and the only way you could keep them under control was by cremating them.

You had a job as a company runner? (Vic was a little deaf and thought he said 'gunner').

Nearly everybody was competent on the machine gun. You had got to be, to be a machine gunner.

The Vickers gun was a piece of mechanical masterpiece really, there was a T-piece with three main stoppages in a machine gun, and you have got to be able to cure those three stoppages in under a minute, to pass as a machine gunner. But usually the machine gunner was an NCO and his number one, that's the bloke who's lay by his side, would help to feed the ammunition for the gun.

I was given the job as company runner. When the lines were down by a barrage or shellfire or the ground was unsuitable for the telephone people to get a line up, the messages had to be taken by hand. If it was on a very tricky front

Seventy years later Vic inspects a similar machine gun at the 80th anniversary of the founding in the Machine Gun Corps in Grantham. Vic was one of three surviving members. The Corps was disbanded in 1922.

there was always two men went in case one got wounded.

You would usually go to the company headquarters which was usually quite primitive and in a big dugout. Then you'd come back to your own regimental or company headquarters, that's where the quartermaster sent all the rations and all that. Beyond the company headquarters was the battalion headquarters or the Brigade headquarters. That's where the people were having a good time. In divisional headquarters, I don't think they ever went through the war without a five-course meal at nights. That might be an exaggeration but is as far as I can ascertain from what I saw.

I think it's very difficult for this modern generation to understand the sheer horror. Looking back you can't describe it. You're asking me these questions, if you had asked me where we were, we didn't know. Take the Battle of the Somme, we didn't know it was the Battle of the Somme, we knew there was a river named the Somme but as far as we were concerned you weren't supposed to know anything really. All you were supposed to know was that Jerry was over there and you're here and you had to stop him getting your bit!

Our world was only what we could see. We didn't know where we were, but it was static warfare from the coast right down to Saint Quentin and right down to where we connected to the French. Every day was a battle. The major battles were the Somme, Thiepval and all that but those weren't day-long battles, the Battle of the Somme lasted nearly twelve months.

On the opening day about 28,000 people lost their lives before breakfast. The bombardment over Jerry's line had lasted the best part of a week with, I think, about five or six miles of wheel-to-wheel artillery, lobbing shells over Jerry's line. After the barrage had finished, the officers said, 'All right, walk forward and take it steady' believing that the German defences had been destroyed. But the defences had not been destroyed and Jerry came out from underground like a lot of rats. That's why the casualties swere so horrific.

The casualties were about 48,000 on the first day and I believe that two-thirds of the casualties could have been avoided. Looking back over the years it was idiotic. To start a battle, the artillery, both Jerry and ours, started a barrage. When the barrage had finished we both knew the infantry was coming, so we had advertised the fact.

It was hushed up actually but records show that during the war there were about 290 people shot for cowardice in the British army. The Americans none, the Australians none, they didn't believe in shooting anybody for cowardice when two-thirds of the cowards were thirty-mile away. It was the biggest tragedy out, that was. We knew it was happening because we came out of trenches early one day, it was about six o'clock in the morning and there was a squad and a kid, he was only about eighteen and we could see the firing party. The tragedy was, that if a bloke spent twelve months in the trenches, got fed up and said, 'Oh well, I've done my share' and he bolted, the military police would pick him up and he would be court-martialled and shot.

What was your worst experience when you were in the front line?

Apart from the initial shock when I was absolutely rigid with fear, I was always afraid of being afraid and that went for a lot of people. I never let anyone see that I was afraid. You overcome it

The worst possible time was the final assault. We had to go without sleep for the 21 days we were behind the German line. Gerry was having his last fling and we held him, we threw every division into the firing line to stop Gerry. The Americans took over our reserve and we knew that we'd held the Germans and the Germans were beaten. We started out with ten of us and we finished up with six. We didn't know where we were, but we broke through and we were all exhausted. We were that damn tired. I always remember, I said to myself,

'I wonder where we are?' and then we saw a cook cart like a NAAFI on wheels with a boiler and tea and soup. We staggered up and the bloke cut me a sandwich, I bet it was about two inches thick,(over 50 millimetres) fantastic! Then the medical man come out from the back of the cart, a doctor or somebody, and he said, 'Don't let him have that, he'll kill himself!'. We had been without food for so long, we had only lived on berries and swedes. I was too damn tired to talk even. Anyway, they put us in a bed of straw and we slept for 24 hours.

When the war finished, that was another memorable day. We had been chasing Jerry and we were near the Franco Belgium border. The weather in France on November 11th was almost identical to that in England, there was a frost, we were all in big greatcoats and everybody's nostrils were blowing vapour out. We were walking up and down and a despatch rider came up to us. Suddenly, bang, a shell landed in a field at the back of us, Jerry was a spiteful devil, it was one minute to eleven. The tragedy was that the Coldstream guards were in that field and I don't know how true it was but later we heard that seven of them had been killed. The despatch rider said, 'It's all over chaps' and we said, 'Get stuffed'.

I spent nearly two years in France. The war finished November 1918 and then there were the assignments on to the Rhine, then we were drawn back to do various fatigues, and it was 1919 when I was demobbed. I had £30 and a suit that didn't fit. Although we were demobbed we were supposed to be on a five-year reserve. They could have called us back at any time.

Of course, when you came back after the First War, you were told that it would be a land fit for kings.

I reckon we had the dirtiest deal that was ever dished out to anybody. It was the same in the Crimean War and the Boer War I suppose. You could say that the last two years of the war was fought by kids from the age of 18 up to 22. They'd served, say, four years in the army. What chance had they got when they came home and there were about six million unemployed munitions workers who had got all the skills? So we were thrown into a saturated market and we hadn't learned anything. I was lucky to get a job at Royal Enfield knocking tacks into footboards on motorcycles. It was a job a monkey could have done if they'd got him to talk. It was a real depression, there are no statistics but I reckon there must have been five million unemployed and no unemployment benefit.

When I first started at the Enfield in 1921, everything was quite primitive. If

Royal Enfield in 1926, as Vic would have known it. This is probably the hub-building section.

you went into the workshops you would see a great many whirling belts driven by overhead pulleys. The girls had to wear caps because if their hair became caught up in a belt they would have been more than scalped. The belts were made from leather and the ends were laced together with metal clips. You had to be careful that you didn't catch the sleeve of your overall in them. Occasionally the clips used to come apart and the belt thrashed dangerously about. We all did our own shoe repairs in those days and we used to try and get hold of a bit of leather belt to resole our shoes. There were still a few of these old belts left in the 1950's. The pulleys were driven by a huge gas engine. It made a terrible noise and was so huge that you had to climb into it. The engine was looked after by Carl Baker, Senior, who kept the Department so spotlessly clean that you could eat your meals off the floor.

The washing facilities at the end of each working period consisted of one bucket brought on to the shop floor. There were thirty-six people on the floor and the thirty-sixth person to use it was washing his hands in a bucket of sludge. However, it wasn't long after the first world war that proper washbasins were installed.

'Teas up'. One of Vic's sketches of factory life. The tea was brought in tin cans by Joe.

Joe

A chap named Ernie Kyte, he taught me a lot about motor bikes, how to do your valve timing and your ignition timing. The Enfield's used to have J A Prestwick engines and they used to come in, just the engine, fly wheels and all that, but the electrics had to be done, you had to put a magneto on, you had the valve assembly and the springs, do the valve timing and the ignition timing for the engine to be put in the frame. I gave him two bob a lesson and I was only getting about 30 bob a week. When I had become proficient I approached the Head of the Motor Cycle Department, George Wakelam, for a job in Assembly, with the vision of a gradual climb upward. I went on engine assembly and from then on I became one of the elite, you know!

I became one of the top managers. I remember one incident when Major Smith, the Managing Director, came to see me one day and said, 'We're having trouble with oval wheels, look into it, will you Vic?'. I knew what he meant. I had heard rumours concerning Cobley Hill near Alvechurch, where a hump-backed bridge goes over a canal, so off I went to see what was going on. Sure enough, there were the young Testers testing the bikes by having a wonderful time. They were riding hard at the bridge, then, as they went over it, they took off, going high into the air and coming down heavily on the other side. This was, of course, making the wheels oval in shape and it had to be stopped.

The motor cycle assembly was very seasonal work, wasn't it?

Well, there were so many companies making motor cycles, you see. I don't know what would have happened if it hadn't been for the Second World War, I reckon somebody must have manipulated the Second World War.

After Whitsun we were often on a three-day week. For the rest of the week you signed on, and went hay-making or fruit-picking. There was nearly a riot in Redditch over that. The flydressers at Alcocks, they were all elite nicely dressed girls,

'Clocking in' at the Royal Enfield factory. You were given a number and had to push the pointer on the bar into your number on arrival and departure. Another of Vic's lightning sketches.

it was a nice decorative arts kind of job. Now, T&M Dixon, had the fruit farms and they had got hop picking and half these girls from Alcocks, were directed to the hop picking. The girls were picking with rag, tag and bobtail from Tipton. There was such an outcry in Redditch, T&M Dixon's name stunk to high heaven.

Holidays were compulsory, when the factory closed down. At first, the holidays were minimal, but as time went on, people had more privileges and the holidays became longer. In the early 1920's, as far as I can remember, we only had a couple of days to cover Christmas and Boxing Day, one day at Easter and two days at Whitsun, plus a week at the August bank holiday. The majority of people couldn't afford to go away and stayed at home or occasionally went on a week-end excursion. We didn't always get our holiday as factories had a rota of workers who were to do an inventory of stores and materials instead. I did not have a holiday for nine years, but did stock-taking to get the extra pay. I didn't mind this because, although each department had its own stores, I changed to another department for stock-taking and I worked for a very nice Storekeeper, Percy Neal, from Astwood Bank, who was very talented and good at his job.

Not long after the first world war, round about 1922, a building next to the Test Shop was adapted as a canteen. It was quite basic and unpretentious, built from corrugated iron rather like a large army hut, and with metal tables and long benches, but it was heated and the Canteen Manageress, Ena Dominick, kept it spotlessly clean. It was open for the lunch break and served meals at midday. It had one area for the staff and another for the workers which was not a reflection on the social divisions of the day but simply because the workers were usually covered in grease which made the benches dirty.

The arrival of a canteen marked a change in attitude by the management who began to show some concern for the welfare of their workers. It also opened up our social lives; workers from different parts of the factory mixed together and, finding mutual interests, formed football teams and other organisations. The canteen was followed by the building of a sports centre.

The workers had little time for leisure but what they had was well provided for. The sports centre included a football field, tennis courts, badminton court and a bowling green (there were eight first class bowling greens in Redditch). The Enfield sports field was one third the length of Windsor Road, opposite the present High Duty Alloys. Each of the large factories provided all these sports facilities for their workers, and each large factory had football, tennis, cricket, bowling and badminton teams. Royal Enfield had three football teams. The factories played matches against each other, usually on Saturday afternoons as we had to work until 12 o'clock on a Saturday. There was a lot of friendly rivalry, particularly between Royal Enfield and the BSA.

I often think how ironic it is that in those days, when they had very little time for leisure, they had all these facilities and now there are so many people out of work who would find them really beneficial they have disappeared.

I went to work at the Austin's for a short period. A lazy place that was, full of corruption, hopeless. Perhaps I felt it was like that because I spent most of my industrial life amongst my own kin. I soon returned to the Enfield.

All the major industries in Redditch had their own fire brigades and in 1939 we knew that war was imminent because and the industries were instructed to form a nucleus across the country of auxiliary fire services.

When the war broke out I was Head Viewer in the motor shop. We were making

Vic Bott with another of his creations, the 'Revelation' small-wheeled bicycle.

motorbikes mostly for the French army but also the English army. I was dissatisfied with the job I was doing. I thought I could do a better job for the war effort and I told that to my boss. If you were in a job that was essential to the war effort, you couldn't leave and the company couldn't sack you but I said that I was going to more or less try to leave the Enfield. Now the government said that eighty odd thousand men had got to be elevated off the shop floor, providing they had the required intelligence, to administrative posts and skilled jobs to help the war effort. Major Smith sent for me, he had a man from the Ministry with him, an elderly scientist. He said to me, 'I want you to take up a new job Bott'. I said, 'Very well'. He said, 'It's all to do with metallurgy' and I said, 'I don't know the first thing about it' and he said, 'That's just what we want'.

Well, the Enfield's had got a contract for making armoured piercing shells and the scientist had to start the APS (army piercing shells) shop. It was all atomic science and metallurgy. I was working with a group of young scientists and the things we had to do! Of course, I had to start again, my maths was hopeless. I was no good at arithmetic, it's part of your set-up. Some parts of your brain refused to function but I made a very good job. These scientists said, any little idea that you think of that has a bearing on a job, no matter how ridiculous it seems, write it down in a book. I filled two books!

Making the shells was a hell of a job. The shell was six inches long and two inches in diameter, a copper driving element was on the base, there was all the silver trace elements at the top and the shelves at the top were pitched with cut glass! It was dire with hardness and it gradually had to be tempered down to soft metal. Now it had to be manufactured to size and longtitudinal flights, it had got to pierce armour two inches thick at an angle of fifteen degrees with sufficient impetus to penetrate tanks and armoured vehicles. We had big ovens with pyrometers, visual pyrometers and mechanical pyrometers, the temperature had to be constant. You'd press the shell in, get it white hot, put it out, quench it, push it down, put it in a rotary temper, and the part that you wanted soft was created by rotating gas.

I sat there at nights, watching, and these chaps were unloading the shells from the ovens and putting them on the floor and you would hear bang, bang, bang! These shells would split just as though you had cut them with a knife. It was like an atomic explosion! It amazed me. These youngsters, they were so brave in handling them. Anyway, I thought that when the shell comes through the tube, you quench it to harden it and then it has got to be tempered with these rotary tempers, and atomic science tells me that there is an inner stress all the time. When they throw them on the floor, something must happen then. How about if we have a rotary roundabout, and as the shell comes out of the furnace, we put it into this roundabout and dip, out, round.

Anyway I designed it and sketched it and one of these scientists came and he took these sketches away and somebody must have worked day and night on it because only a week later he come in with this beautiful little roundabout with a timing device, the shell was never in that atmosphere for so many seconds. Cured it! Tommy Guise flew to America to help them, they were in a terrible mess with their armour piercing shells.

I was responsible for other technical inventions, for example I helped in the development of a telescopic fork on the motor bike, but the revolution of instantaneous tempering for the hardening process so that the shell never fractured was my major achievement.

The fascinating thing is that you were able to sketch this. Your sketching and drawing ability is well known in Redditch. In 1946, when you were 46 years old, you achieved a life-time ambition by having a job that you really liked. How did this come about?

On the cessation of hostilities the 2 lb anti-tank shell department closed and I was asked what other job I would like. As I had always wanted to be a draughtsman, I told the management that I would like to go into the Drawing Office. I was therefore very pleased to become a draughtsman in the Jig and Tool Drawing Office.

One of the peculiarities of Royal Enfield at that time was that you were expected to turn your hand to a number of skills. When I worked on the factory floor I was often called into the Drawing Office to help out. When I settled in the Drawing Office, I became the works' unofficial artist. I drew exploded isometric illustrations

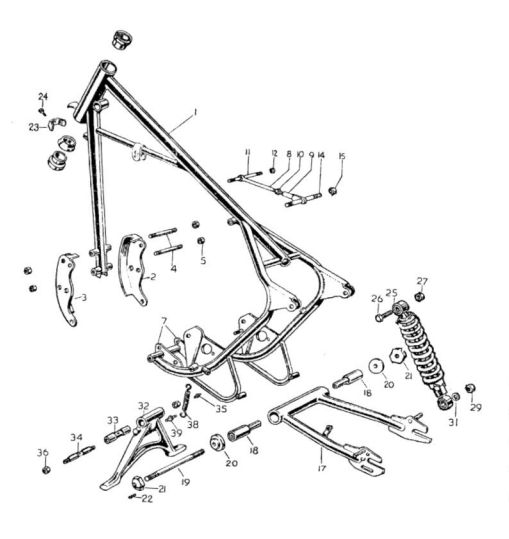

One of Vic's exploded diagrams for part of a bicycle frame. Most of them were far more complex.

for the workshop manuals (such as the list of spare and replacement parts for the 1965 Continental GT) and I designed motor cycle tank motifs. In about 1952, I was asked to design the wing motif which was used on the Bullet, one for the left-hand side and one for the right. Afterwards the management decided that they wanted just the one which they could put on either side, so the wing had to be redesigned. I remember that we employed a Senior Draughtsman from the Austin Company, and he was asked to design a jig for the borematic machine, which is basic design operation. To my astonishment he was unable to do it. He explained that at Austin's, there was such a high division of labour that he only did the one drilling fixture.

I was 68 when I retired, I went three years over like the train robbers. I spent the last three years with E&HP Smith, it was a cushy job and well paid.

When you came back to Redditch after the First World War you got very much involved with the British Legion.

We had quite a job to start the British Legion but when we did, we had some very good people. Colonel Scothern, Major Smith, Harry Blackford, Colonel Milward, they were the instigators, they started the ball rolling. RWSmith had all three sons serve in the Redditch artillery, Major Smith was second in command of the battery's, George was a second lieutenant, Stanley was a second lieutenant, he was really committed to the cause. Then there was myself, a chap named Sid Smith and a chap named George Wiggett, we were the first three signatures on the committee. RW Smith, let us have a Masonic Lodge in Easemore Road on a peppercorn rent with a promise that we should have it if we behaved ourselves. It's now the British Legion club.

You have seen it all, Vic. You have seen things move at the speed of a horse, now to things that move at the speed of jet travel. People have gone to the moon.

When the war broke out, all the Fire Brigades were under the voluntary fire service. Now part of our duty at night was aircraft spotting. We were on the top of our offices that were three-stories high, and I was with a kid named Wally Powell, a smashing kid he was, proper country lad but he had got a brain and a half. We were watching an aircraft, we had just spotted it in the moonlight, I don't know whether it was ours or theirs, then it disappeared, and Wally said, 'The buggers gone behind the moon!'. I said, 'What?'. I nearly fell off the roof . You know, technology was advancing so rapidly I wouldn't have been surprised if it had gone behind the moon. It was only four or five years later they'd got a car, a buggy, up there. How ridiculous can you get in this modern age?

And you've seen Redditch grow from a small country town to a town now of 80 or 90 thousand. What do you think about it?

Well, it has its drawbacks but I should say that it is a distinct improvement. Redditch was falling to bits, a lot of the property was very old.

I always remember Redditch has the reputation of Redditch having a little jewel – St Stephen's church and the churchyard. My cousin used to come up from Cheltenham and he'd say they haven't got anything like this in their town centre. I think there are 22 species of trees in that enclosure and on a summer's day you can sit there and see St Stephen's Church. Marvelous, you know.

I like Redditch, I reckon Redditch has got character, well when you come to weigh it up, Redditch was in the 50 mile radius that revolutionised the world. The industrial age started within a 50 mile radius of where we are, at Ironbridge.

I think that's a marvelous way to end this very enlightening and interesting talk with you, Vic.